Why Must I...

Brush my Teeth?

Jackie Gaff

**Photography by
Chris Fairclough**

CHERRYTREE BOOKS

A Cherrytree book

First published by
Evans Brothers Ltd
2A Portman Mansions
Chiltern Street
London W1U 6NR

Reprinted 2006, 2008

British Library Cataloguing in Publication Data
Gaff, Jackie
   Why Must I brush my teeth?
   1.Teeth - Care and hygiene - Juvenile literature 2.Health - Juvenile literature
   I.Title
   617.6'01

978 1 84234 258 9

Planned and produced by Discovery Books Ltd
Editor: Helena Attlee
Designer: Ian Winton
Illustrator: Joanna Williams
Consultants: Pat Jackson, Professional Officer for School Nursing, The Community Practitioners' and
Health Visitors' Association. Rachel Hope BDS (Hons) MFDSRCSEd

Acknowledgements
The author and publisher would like to thank the following for kind permission to reproduce photographs:
Corbis: p20 (Strauss/Curtis/Corbis), p26 (Rolf Bruderer/Corbis).
Commissioned photography by Chris Fairclough.
The author, packager and publisher would like to thank the following people for their participation in the
book: Alice Baldwin-Hay, Lucy Boyd, Harry Hinton Boyd, Charlotte and William Cooper, the staff and
pupils of Presteigne County Primary School, Rachel Hope and the staff of the Dental Practice, Hay-on-Wye.

Contents

Why must I brush my teeth?

Dirty teeth look horrible, and they can cause toothache. Brushing keeps your teeth and your gums clean and healthy.

You need your teeth for eating and talking. Try to say 'th' without putting the tip of your tongue against your teeth.

Where would you be without teeth? You would not be able to bite into food, let alone chew it!

First toothbrushes

Toothbrushes with bristles were invented in China about 500 years ago. The bristles were made from pigs' hair.

If you don't brush your teeth you might get holes in them. Big holes give you bad toothache.

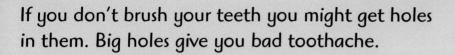

Even tiny holes can make your teeth ache when you eat something very hot or very cold.

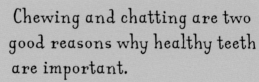

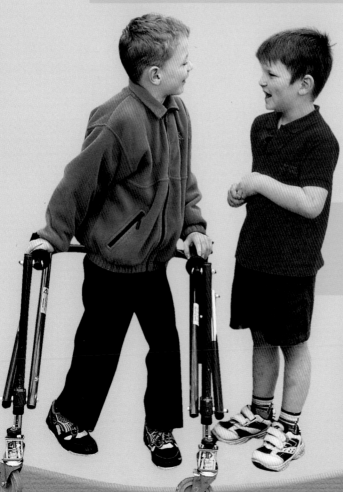

Chewing and chatting are two good reasons why healthy teeth are important.

Dirty teeth can give you bad breath. No one likes getting too close to someone whose breath is smelly — so go on, get out your toothbrush!

Brushwork

Even the tiniest scrap of food can harm your teeth. Here is the best way to keep them squeaky clean.

Take the cap off the toothpaste. Squeeze the tube gently from the bottom to put paste on your brush. You don't need a lot — just a pea-sized lump.

Wet your brush under the cold tap. Now, brush gently along the sides of your teeth, making circular movements with the brush.

Brush your front teeth and the outside edge of your other teeth.

Keep the circles moving slowly along all your teeth, inside and out.

When you've done the sides, brush backwards and forwards along the tops of your teeth.

Take your time – try to brush for about three minutes. When you're done, spit out all the toothpaste.

HEALTHY HINTS

- Clean your teeth at least twice a day, after breakfast and before going to bed.

- Be gentle – don't scrub your teeth.

- Get a new toothbrush every two to three months.

- Ask a grown-up to check that you are cleaning your teeth properly.

Don't forget to rinse your brush when you've finished.

All about toothpaste

Toothpaste cleans your teeth and protects them against harmful germs.

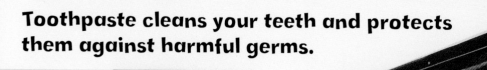

Most toothpastes contains small amounts of a **chemical** called **fluoride**. It helps to strengthen and protect your teeth.

There are lots of different kinds of toothpaste, but they all do the same job.

Fluoride is often added to tap water because scientists have found that it protects teeth.

Only use a little toothpaste, and try not to swallow it while you are brushing.

Toothpaste contains a kind of foamy soap, and a material like finely powdered chalk. The foam rinses the **germs** off your teeth, and the chalk helps to rub off anything that is stuck to your teeth.

If you are thirsty, drink before brushing - it's best not to rinse the fluoride away.

9

Flossing

Tooth floss is a waxy string that you can use to clean between your teeth.

Flossing your teeth is easy, but you must do it very gently and carefully.

Use a piece of floss about 25 cm long. Wrap the ends around the middle fingers of each hand, leaving about 9 cm spare in the middle.

Stretch the floss tight, then gently slip it down between two teeth. Pull it up and down a few times between the tooth and your **gum**.

Pull the floss tight between your fingers.

Carry on flossing until you've cleaned between all your teeth, top and bottom. When you've finished, rinse your mouth out with clean water.

Floss your teeth very gently, so that you don't hurt your gums.

HEALTHY HINTS

- Floss your teeth every day.
- Do not pull floss so hard that it cuts your gums.

11

Cutting and chewing

You need strong teeth to break food down so that you can swallow it.

Take a look inside your mouth. Can you see that your teeth have different shapes? Each shape is designed to do a particular job.

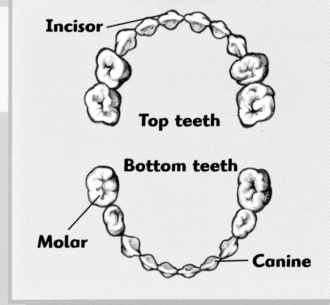

Incisor

Top teeth

Bottom teeth

Molar

Canine

This diagram shows the different kinds of teeth in your mouth.

Your eight front teeth (four top and four bottom) are called **incisors**. Their job is cutting and slicing food.

Your eight front teeth have a sharp, straight, cutting edge.

Big mouth!

You might expect the world's biggest animal to have the world's biggest teeth. But the blue whale doesn't have teeth at all. It sieves its food through huge, fringed mouth-brushes called baleen.

The pointy teeth next to your incisors are called **canines**. They are for cutting and tearing.

Your back teeth have broad, lumpy tops. They are called **molars**. Their job is grinding up food until it is small enough for you to swallow.

You use your incisors to bite off a mouthful of food and your molars to chew it up.

You would use your molars to grind up this delicious, crunchy salad.

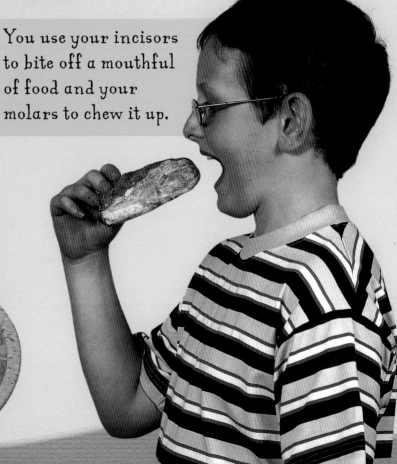

How tough are teeth?

Teeth are made up of three layers. They are **hard** on the outside but **soft** in the middle.

This is what the inside of a tooth looks like.

The layers of **enamel** and **dentine** on the outside of your teeth work like armour to protect the sensitive **pulp** in the middle of your tooth.

Pulp is packed with **blood** vessels and **nerves**. The blood vessels feed the tooth.

Enamel
The toughest material in your whole body!

Pulp
Soft and sensitive.

Gum

Dentine
Not as tough as the enamel, but it is still as hard as bone.

Nerves and blood vessels

Fossil teeth
Because teeth are so hard, they are often discovered thousands of years after a human or animal has died.

Gum shield

The nerves carry messages to your brain. They tell you that ice-cream is cold, or warn you when soup is too hot. Nerves also tell you when things hurt, like toothache!

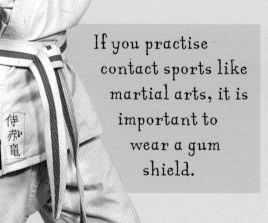

If you practise contact sports like martial arts, it is important to wear a gum shield.

HEALTHY HINTS

- Do not brush your teeth too hard.
- Never bite on very hard things like nutshells.
- Wear a gum shield when you play contact sports.

Germ attack

When teeth aren't brushed properly, a sticky coating called plaque builds up on them.

Plaque is the home of germs that attack teeth. They belong to a germ group called **bacteria**.

Like all germs, bacteria are so tiny that they can only be seen under a **microscope**.

Plaque bacteria feast on the food scraps they find on your teeth and gums. As they feed, they produce an **acid** so tough that it rots tooth enamel and makes a hole in it. This is called a **cavity**.

How a cavity forms

Plaque bacteria eat any food scraps left on your teeth.

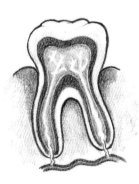

Acid in the bacteria creates a small hole called a cavity.

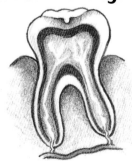

Left untreated, the cavity will gradually grow larger and larger.

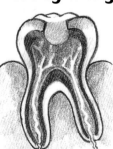

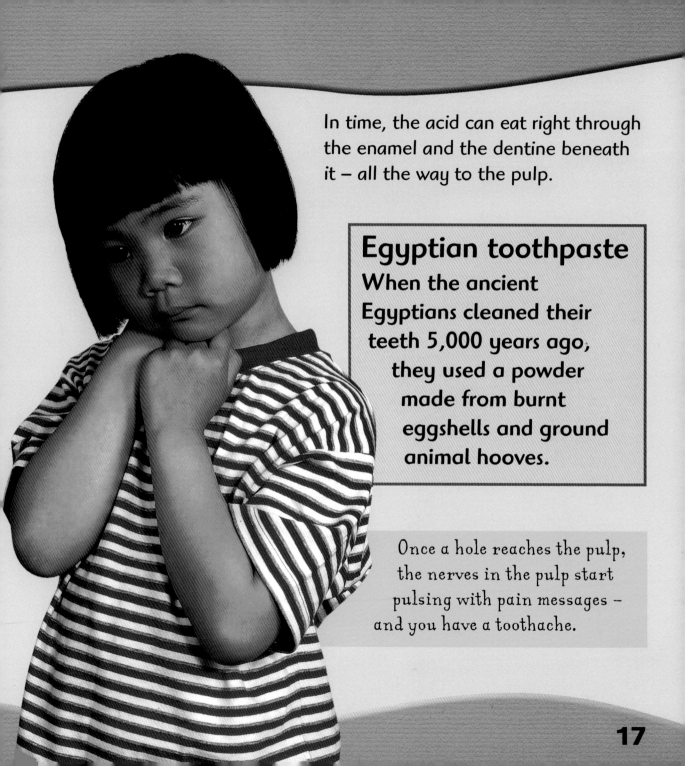

In time, the acid can eat right through the enamel and the dentine beneath it – all the way to the pulp.

Egyptian toothpaste

When the ancient Egyptians cleaned their teeth 5,000 years ago, they used a powder made from burnt eggshells and ground animal hooves.

Once a hole reaches the pulp, the nerves in the pulp start pulsing with pain messages – and you have a toothache.

Sweet tooth

**Do you like sweets? So do plaque bacteria!
They use sugar to make the acid that eats
holes in your teeth.**

Sugary food includes puddings, cakes and
biscuits as well as sweets. Harmful acids form
in your mouth every
time you eat them.

Instead of eating sweets and biscuits,
why not try fresh or dried fruit?

Fizzy drinks, concentrated fruit juice
and squash all contain lots of sugar.

Some sweets are worse than others. Toffee takes a long time to chew. This means that it leaves lots of sugar on your teeth.

The only time to eat sugary food is after a main meal. Then the **saliva** in your mouth helps to wash the sugar away. The worst time to have it is as a snack between meals.

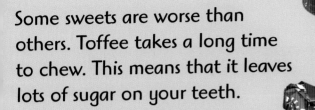

HEALTHY HINTS

- Snack on fruit instead of sugary food or drink.
- Try to clean your teeth after eating sweet things.
- If you can't brush your teeth after eating sweet things, rinse your mouth out with water.

Wobbly teeth

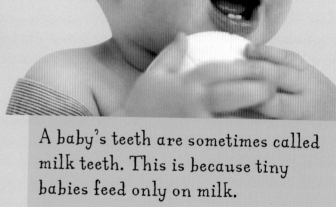

Have you got a wobbly tooth? Baby teeth wobble when they are loose and ready to fall out.

You will only have two sets of teeth in your life. The first ones are called baby teeth. This is because they started to appear when you were a baby.

A baby's teeth are sometimes called milk teeth. This is because tiny babies feed only on milk.

Your second set of teeth are called permanent teeth. Permanent teeth start to replace your baby teeth when you are six or seven years old.

Permanent teeth may take a little while to fill the gaps in your mouth.

Permanent teeth have to last you forever. If they fall out, new ones won't grow to replace them.

Viking tooth fairy

Do you believe in the tooth fairy? The story may date back to Viking times, when people celebrated the loss of baby teeth by giving children a gift.

The last four teeth to arrive are called wisdom teeth, even though they have nothing to do with braininess. Some people never get wisdom teeth, but others start to get them in their late teens.

Look after your permanent teeth - they need to last a lifetime!

Visiting the dentist

To keep teeth in tip-top condition, you should visit the dentist at least twice a year.

A grown-up must ring the dentist to make an appointment. This is a particular time that the dentist can see you.

The receptionist at the surgery makes the appointments.

On the day of your appointment, the receptionist will greet you when you arrive. You will sit in a waiting room until it is your turn to go into the dentist's surgery. There are usually some books and toys to keep you busy while you wait.

HEALTHY HINTS

- Visit the dentist for a check up every six months.

- Help yourself and the dentist by looking after your teeth properly between visits.

Your name will be called by the dental nurse when the dentist is ready for you. The nurse helps the dentist while she or he looks at your teeth.

You must arrive at the surgery on time, or you might miss your appointment.

Drilling and filling

The dentist has a special chair. She can make it go up and down, and tip it backwards.

The dentist's bright light helps her to see into your mouth.

The dentist needs to look at each of your teeth very carefully. If plaque bacteria are eating a hole in one of your teeth, you may need a **filling**.

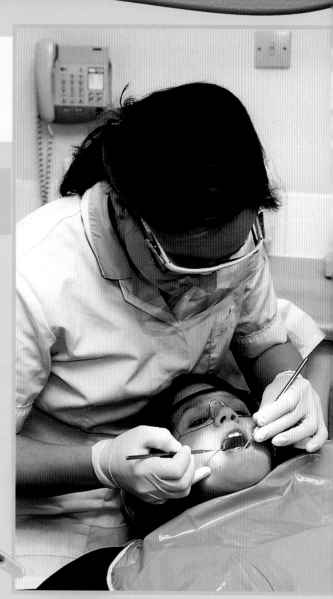

This mirror on a long, metal handle makes it easier for the dentist to look at your teeth.

Any rotting bits of tooth must be cleaned away with a tiny drill. When the hole is clean, the dentist will fill it with tooth-coloured **cement**.

Plaque bacteria have eaten a hole in this molar.

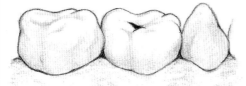

The dentist uses a drill to clear out the hole.

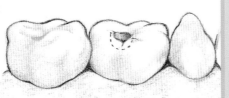

The new filling is almost invisible.

The first dentists

Specially trained dentists have only been around for about 150 years. Before then, barbers not only gave haircuts, they also treated people's toothache!

The filling will protect your tooth and stop it hurting. Soon, you will hardly know that your filling is there.

Bracing up

Sometimes permanent teeth grow too far apart or too close together.

If this happens you may need to see a special dentist called an **orthodontist**.

Orthodontists use braces to correct the position of teeth. A brace is made from brackets and thin metal wire.

The brackets are fixed to the teeth, and then the wire is threaded through the brackets to move the teeth gently into the correct position.

Everyone's mouth and teeth are different, so you might need a brace for anything from a few months to a couple of years.

A brace can feel a bit strange at first, but it won't take long to get used to it. Don't worry – it works very gently and slowly, so you won't feel your teeth moving.

When the orthodontist takes the brace off, you will have a brilliant set of beautiful teeth!

It is more difficult to keep your teeth clean when you have a brace. A fluoride **mouthwash** will help to keep your teeth and gums clean and healthy.

Keep on smiling!

Dogs wag their tails if they are pleased to see you. Cats purr and humans smile.

A smile isn't nearly so nice if your teeth are dirty. Clean teeth look good and they are also stronger and healthier.

Smiling is catching – have you noticed how people usually smile back when you greet them with a big grin?

Clean teeth are also better at fighting off the plaque bacteria that are itching to eat holes in them and give you toothache.

Strong, healthy teeth are less likely to be worn down by a lifetime of eating.

What is the best way to keep your teeth clean? Brushing and flossing, of course!

HEALTHY HINTS

- **Brush your teeth at least twice a day.**

- **Try to floss every night before bedtime.**

- **Visit the dentist every six months.**

Glossary

Acid
The acid produced by plaque bacteria eats holes in teeth.

Bacteria
Bacteria are tiny, living things that can only be seen through a microscope.

Blood vessel
A tube through which blood flows.

Canines
The pointy teeth next to your incisors.

Cavity
The hole that bacteria can make in your tooth.

Cement
A paste-like material used by dentists to fill holes in your teeth.

Chemicals
The substances that make up the world's materials.

Dentine
The second layer of the tooth, between the enamel and the pulp.

Enamel
The hard coating on the outside of teeth.

Filling
A hard material used to pack a hole in a tooth.

Floss
A fine, wax-coated string, which you use to clean in the gaps between your teeth.

Fluoride
A chemical which is added to toothpaste and water supplies because scientists have found that it helps teeth to fight decay, or rotting.

Germ
A tiny living thing that causes disease.

Gum
The firm, shiny pink skin that covers your jaws and the roots of your teeth.

Incisors
Your front teeth – you have two in your top jaw and two in your bottom jaw.

Microscope
A device in which lenses are used to magnify objects.

Molars
Your back teeth – the ones with broad, lumpy tops.

Mouthwash
A germ-killing liquid which people use to help keep their mouths clean.

Nerve
Nerves carry messages from your brain to every part of your body, telling it about things like heat, cold and pain.

Orthodontist
A dentist who specializes in helping teeth to grow straight and even.

Plaque
A thin, sticky film that can build up on teeth if they are not brushed and flossed properly to keep them clean.

Pulp
The soft, sensitive material at the centre of the tooth.

Saliva
A liquid that your mouth produces to help protect your teeth by rinsing away food scraps and harmful germs.

Further resources

Websites

www.canadianparents.com
A lively, interactive website offering advice and information on all aspects of family life, including health and hygiene.

www.dentalhealth.org.uk
British Dental Health Foundation website, offering advice and information on all aspects of dentistry.

www.kidshealth.org
American, child-centred site devoted to all aspects of health and wellbeing. Includes advice on taking care of teeth and banishing bad breath.

www.nzda.org.nz
New Zealand Dental Association website.

www.wholefamily.com
A question and answer type website concerned with all aspects of American family life. Includes tips on persuading reluctant 7-year-olds to brush their teeth.

Books

Healthy Teeth, Angela Royston, Heinemann Library, 2003.

Look After Yourself: Your Teeth, Claire Llewellyn, Franklin Watts, 2002.

My Amazing Body: Staying Healthy, Angela Royston, Raintree, 2004.

Sam's Science: I Know Why I Brush My Teeth, Kate Rowan, Walker Books, 1999.

Index